1791

The Massachusetts Historical Society is an independent research library that collects, preserves, makes accessible, and communicates manuscripts and other materials that promote the study of the history of Massachusetts and the nation—a mission it has pursued since 1791.

COLLECTING HISTORY

Building of the Massachusetts Historical Society

Massachusetts Historical Society

ISBN: 0-934909-95-4
ISBN: 978-0-934909-95-2

Printed in the United States of America by
RR Donnelley, W.E. Andrews Plant, Bedford, Massachusetts 01730.

Designed by Jeffrey Williamson.

Photography of historical objects by John Holt, Dock 25, Boston, Massachusetts.

Cover:
Christian Remick. Perspective View of the Blockad[e] of Boston Harbour, circa 1768.
From the estate of Henry Lee Shattuck, 1970.

Inside front cover:
Thomas Jefferson. The Declaration of Independence. Manuscript copy, 1776.
Gift of Mr. and Mrs. Alexander C. Washburn, 1893.

DOCUMENTS IN INTRODUCTION:

Title page: Photograph of the Massachusetts Historical Society building, 1918.

Massachusetts Historical Society. Circular Letter, of the Historical Society,
1 November 1791. From the Massachusetts Historical Society Archives.

Paul Revere. Letter to Jeremy Belknap, Corresponding Secretary of the Massachusetts
Historical Society, 1 January 1798. From the Massachusetts Historical Society Archives.

CHAPTER HEADING DECORATIONS:

Chapter I
Signatures of John Adams, Thomas Jefferson, and John Quincy Adams.

Chapter II
Officer's small sword owned by John Thomas, anonymous European maker,
circa 1730-1740. From the estate of William A. Thomas, 1904.

Chapter III
Shem Drowne. Indian Archer Weathervane, circa 1716.
Gift of Emily Warren Appleton, 1876.

Chapter IV
John Singleton Copley. Untitled sketch of a rose, circa 1753.
Probably the gift of Frederic Amory, 1921.

Inside back cover:
James Brown Marston. State Street, 1801.
Purchased by subscription, 1879.

CONTENTS

CIRCULAR LETTER,

OF THE

HISTORICAL SOCIETY.

SIR,

A SOCIETY has lately been inftituted in this town, called the HISTORICAL SOCIETY; the profeffed defign
of which is, to collect, preferve and communicate, materials
for a complete hiftory of this country, and accounts of all
valuable efforts of human ingenuity and induftry, from the
beginning of its fettlement. In purfuance of this plan, they
have already amaffed a large quantity of books, pamphlets,
and manuscripts; and are ftill in fearch of more: A cata-
logue of which will be printed for the information of the
public.

THEY have alfo given encouragement to the publication of
a weekly paper, to be called THE AMERICAN APOLLO;
in which will be given the refult of their inquiries, into the natural, political and ecclefiaftical hiftory of this country. A propofal for the printing of this paper is here in-
clofed to you; and it is requefted that you would promote
fubfcriptions for it; and contribute to its value and importance, by attention to the articles annexed. The Society

beg

Acknowledgments

Donors have made the Massachusetts Historical Society one of the greatest repositories of our nation's past. Few have holdings that can match the MHS in quality and significance. This publication celebrates the foresight, caring, and generosity of those individuals.

One especially generous donor, Peter Spang, needs to be recognized for his ongoing commitment and contributions to the Society. A trustee for many years, he has served as a vice president and the chair of the Collections Committee. His dedication to the Society exemplifies the tradition of giving that these pages illustrate. It is a very generous gift from Peter that has made publication of this compendium possible. He has our deepest gratitude.

We are indebted to David McCullough, a longtime friend of the MHS, for writing the foreword to this publication and supporting us in countless other ways. Peter Drummey, Stephen T. Riley Librarian, prepared the text, drawing on his encyclopedic knowledge of our collection. His cohort, Anne Bentley, our Curator of Art, added her expertise and project oversight. I also want to thank Brenda Lawson, Director of Collections Services; Mary Fabiszewski, Senior Cataloger; Nancy Heywood, Digital Projects Coordinator; Ondine Le Blanc, Director of Publications; Jeanine Rees, Assistant Editor; and Nicole Leonard, Associate Director of Development, for their contributions.

Well into its third century, the Massachusetts Historical Society takes this opportunity to share its riches with an ever widening audience and—we hope—a future generation of donors.

Dennis A. Fiori
President

Dear Sir,
Having a little leisure, I wish to
promise of giving you some facts, & Anecdotes
the Battle of Lexington, which I do not remember
any history of the American Revolution.

In the year 1773 I was imployed by the Se-
lectmen of Boston to carry the Account of the Destruction of the
Tea to New-york, & afterwards, 1774, to carry their
New-york & Philadelphia, for calling a Congress;
Congress, several times. In the Fall of 1774 & Winter
one of upwards of thirty, chiefly mechanics, who formed our selves
for the purpose of watching the movements of the
& gaining every inteligence in the movements of the
held our meetings, at the Green Dragon,
our meetings should be kept secret; that every time
person swore upon the Bible, that they would not
our transactions, but, to Messrs. Hancock, Adams, Doctors Warren,
& one or two more. About November, when things
serious, a Gentleman who had conections with the
a Whig at heart, acquainted me, that our meetings were
mentioned the words, identical, that were spoken among
before, We did not then distrust Dr. Church, but
some one among us. We removed to another pla
was more secure; but here we found that all our
were communicated to Govr. Gage. (This come to
then Secretary Flucker, He told it to the Gentlemen mentioned
then a common opinion, that there was a Traytor in
ness & that Gage was possessed of all their secrets. (Church
of that Congress for Boston.) In the Winter, towards the
quently took Turns, two & two, to watch the Soldiers,
all night.
the Streets. The Saturday night preceding the 19th
oclock at Night, the Boats belonging to the transport
launched, & carried under the sterns of the men of War,
previously hauld up & repaired). We likewise found

Foreword

There is simply nothing to compare to reading the original letters, diaries, and manuscripts of the American story, to hold the real thing in your own hands, the letters of John and Abigail Adams, for example, or of Thomas Jefferson. There is a tangible, tactile thrill one feels that no words can adequately describe. It is as close to those vanished people and their times as you can get, and the collections of such treasures at the Massachusetts Historical Society, all under one roof, are like none to be found anywhere else.

It would be hard for me to say which of those documents that I have worked with is my favorite. I love John Adams's famous letter to Abigail in which he so clearly understands the immense importance of the vote for independence cast on 2 July 1776 at the Continental Congress, but in which he also predicts the fanfare Independence Day will be given down the years, and foresees a vast continental nation besides. But then there are more than a thousand other letters between John and Abigail to choose from, and neither was capable of being dull or writing briefly.

As for the letters between Adams and Jefferson in their post-presidential years, they rank among the most remarkable in American history or, for that matter, in the English language. Still, I have to say the morning I first saw Paul Revere's own account of his historic night ride before Lexington and Concord was one I will never forget.

How wonderful that this handsome sampling of the full range of the treasures at hand has been provided now for so many to read and enjoy.

David McCullough

to be understood, would require more time and thought than I can possibly Spare. It is not indeed the fine Arts, which our Country requires. — the Usefull, the mechanic Arts, are those which We have occasion for in a young Country, as yet Simple and not far advanced in Luxury, altho perhaps much too far for her Age and Character. —

I could fill Volumes with Descriptions of Temples and Palaces, Paintings, Sculptures, Tapestry, Porcelaine, &c &c &c. — if I could have time. but I could not do this without neglecting my duty. — The Science of Government it is my Duty to study, more than all other Sciences — the Art of Legislation and Administration and Negotiation, ought to take Place, indeed to exclude in a manner all other Arts. — I must study Politicks and War that my Sons may have liberty to study Painting and Poetry Mathematicks and Philosophy. — my Sons ought to study Mathematicks and Philosophy, Geography, natural History and Naval Architecture, navigation, Commerce and Agriculture, in order to give their Children a right to study Painting, Poetry, Musick, Architecture, Statuary, Tapestry, and Porcelaine. —

Adieu.

Introduction

The Massachusetts Historical Society holds more than 3,600 collections of personal and family papers—an unparalleled resource for the study of American history from the colonial period through the twentieth century. At the heart of its collections are the personal papers of three presidents, John and John Quincy Adams and Thomas Jefferson. Examples of their manuscripts, together with a letter from the irrepressible Abigail Adams, form the first section of this guide.

The remaining three sections are arranged according to the educational scheme that John Adams set out in a letter to Abigail in 1780. For the benefit of future generations, he wrote,

> *I must study Politicks and War that my Sons may have liberty to study Mathematicks and Philosophy. my Sons ought to study Mathematicks and Philosophy, Geography, natural History Naval Architecture, navigation, Commerce and Agriculture, in order to give their Children a right to study Painting Poetry Musick, Architecture, Statuary, Tapestry and Porcelaine.*

In the three sections that follow, "Politics & War" tells the political and military history of the United States through personal papers and artifacts. The second section, "Mathematics & Philosophy, Navigation & Commerce," covers the broad sweep of American social and business history. The final section, "Painting, Poetry, & Architecture," contains examples from the Society's art collection, as well as the writings and drawings of authors and artists.

John Adams. Letter to Abigail Adams, post 12 May 1780.
Gift of the Adams Manuscript Trust, 1956.

John

Thielke

John Qui

THE PERSONAL PAPERS OF
THREE PRESIDENTS

Miss Adorable

By the Same Token
that the Bearer hereof satt up with
you last night I hereby order you
to give him, as many Kisses, and
as many Hours of your Company
after 9 O'Clock as he shall please
to Demand and and charge them to
my Account: This Order, or Requisition
call it which you will is in Consi
deration of a similar order Upon Aurelia
for the like favour, and I presume I have
good Right to draw upon you for the Kisses
as I have given two or three Millions
at least, when one has been received and of
Consequence the Account between us is
immensely in favour of yours

Octr 4th 1762   John Adams

John Adams ~ Letter to Abigail Adams

4 OCTOBER 1762   Gift of the Adams Manuscript Trust, 1956.

The courtship of John and Abigail Adams is chronicled by correspondence that began with a facetious contract written three years after they met. "Miss Adorable," her admiring lawyer addresses her,

> *By the same Token that the Bearer hereof satt up with you last night I hereby order you to give him, as many Kisses, and as many Hours of your Company after 9 O Clock as he shall please to Demand and charge them to my Account.*

The 1,200 letters exchanged by Abigail and John Adams form the cornerstone of the Adams Family Papers—the largest and most important manuscript collection held by the Historical Society.

Benjamin Blyth ~ John Adams and Abigail Adams, circa 1766.
Gift of John Adams, a great-great-grandson of the sitters, 1957.

In CONGRESS, July 4, 1776.

A DECLARATION

By the REPRESENTATIVES of the

UNITED STATES OF AMERICA,

In GENERAL CONGRESS ASSEMBLED.

WHEN in the Course of human Events, it becomes neceſſary for one People to diſſolve the Political Bands which have connected them with another, and to aſſume among the Powers of the Earth, the ſeparate and equal Station to which the Laws of Nature and of Nature's God entitle them, a decent Reſpect to the Opinions of Mankind requires that they ſhould declare the cauſes which impel them to the Separation.

We hold theſe Truths to be ſelf-evident, that all Men are created equal, that they are endowed by their Creator with certain unalienable Rights, that among theſe are Life, Liberty, and the Purſuit of Happineſs---That to ſecure theſe Rights, Governments are inſtituted among Men, deriving their juſt Powers from the Conſent of the Governed, that whenever any Form of Government becomes deſtructive of theſe Ends, it is the Right of the People to alter or to aboliſh it, and to inſtitute new Government, laying its Foundation on ſuch Principles, and organizing its Powers in ſuch Form, as to them ſhall ſeem moſt likely to effect their Safety and Happineſs. Prudence, indeed, will dictate that Governments long eſtabliſhed ſhould not be changed for light and tranſient Cauſes; and accordingly all Experience hath ſhewn, that Mankind are more diſpoſed to ſuffer, while Evils are ſufferable, than to right themſelves by aboliſhing the Forms to which they are accuſtomed. But when a long Train of Abuſes and Uſurpations, purſuing invariably the ſame Object, evinces a Deſign to reduce them under abſolute Deſpotiſm, it is their Right, it is their Duty, to throw off ſuch Government, and to provide new Guards for their future Security. Such has been the patient Sufferance of theſe Colonies; and ſuch is now the Neceſſity which conſtrains them to alter their former Syſtems of Government. The Hiſtory of the preſent King of Great-Britain is a Hiſtory of repeated Injuries and Uſurpations, all having in direct Object the Eſtabliſhment of an abſolute Tyranny over theſe States. To prove this, let Facts be ſubmitted to a candid World.

He has refuſed his Aſſent to Laws, the moſt wholeſome and neceſſary for the public Good.

He has forbidden his Governors to paſs Laws of immediate and preſſing Importance, unleſs ſuspended in their Operation till his Aſſent ſhould be obtained; and when ſo ſuspended, he has utterly neglected to attend to them.

He has refuſed to paſs other Laws for the Accommodation of large Diſtricts of People, unleſs thoſe People would relinquiſh the Right of Repreſentation in the Legiſlature, a Right ineſtimable to them, and formidable to Tyrants only.

He has called together Legiſlative Bodies at Places unuſual, uncomfortable, and diſtant from the Depoſitory of their public Records, for the ſole Purpoſe of fatiguing them into Compliance with his Meaſures.

He has diſſolved Repreſentative Houſes repeatedly, for oppoſing with manly Firmneſs his Invaſions on the Rights of the People.

He has refuſed for a long Time, after ſuch Diſſolutions, to cauſe others to be elected; whereby the Legiſlative Powers, incapable of Annihilation, have returned to the People at large for their exerciſe; the State remaining in the mean time expoſed to all the Dangers of Invaſion from without, and Convulſions within.

He has endeavoured to prevent the Population of theſe States; for that Purpoſe obſtructing the Laws for Naturalization of Foreigners; refuſing to paſs others to encourage their Migrations hither, and raiſing the Conditions of new Appropriations of Lands.

He has obſtructed the Adminiſtration of Juſtice, by refuſing his Aſſent to Laws for eſtabliſhing Judiciary Powers.

He has made Judges dependent on his Will alone, for the Tenure of their Offices, and the Amount and Payment of their Salaries.

He has erected a Multitude of new Offices, and ſent hither Swarms of Officers to harraſs our People, and eat out their Subſtance.

He has kept among us, in Times of Peace, Standing Armies, without the conſent of our Legiſlatures.

He has affected to render the Military independent of and ſuperior to the Civil Power.

He has combined with others to ſubject us to a Juriſdiction foreign to our Conſtitution, and unacknowledged by our Laws; giving his Aſſent to their Acts of pretended Legiſlation:

For quartering large Bodies of Armed Troops among us:

For protecting them, by a mock Trial, from Puniſhment for any Murders which they ſhould commit on the Inhabitants of theſe States:

For cutting off our Trade with all Parts of the World:

For impoſing Taxes on us without our Conſent:

For depriving us, in many Caſes, of the Benefits of Trial by Jury:

For tranſporting us beyond Seas to be tried for pretended Offences:

For aboliſhing the free Syſtem of Engliſh Laws in a neighbouring Province, eſtabliſhing therein an arbitrary Government, and enlarging its Boundaries, ſo as to render it at once an Example and fit Inſtrument for introducing the ſame abſolute Rule into theſe Colonies:

For taking away our Charters, aboliſhing our moſt valuable Laws, and altering fundamentally the Forms of our Governments:

For ſuspending our own Legiſlatures, and declaring themſelves inveſted with Power to legiſlate for us in all Caſes whatſoever.

He has abdicated Government here, by declaring us out of his Protection and waging War againſt us.

He has plundered our Seas, ravaged our Coaſts, burnt our Towns, and deſtroyed the Lives of our People.

He is, at this Time, tranſporting large Armies of foreign Mercenaries to compleat the Works of Death, Deſolation, and Tyranny, already begun with circumſtances of Cruelty and Perfidy, ſcarcely paralleled in the moſt barbarous Ages, and totally unworthy the Head of a civilized Nation.

He has conſtrained our fellow Citizens taken Captive on the high Seas to bear Arms againſt their Country, to become the Executioners of their Friends and Brethren, or to fall themſelves by their Hands.

He has excited domeſtic Inſurrections amongſt us, and has endeavoured to bring on the Inhabitants of our Frontiers, the mercileſs Indian Savages, whoſe known Rule of Warfare, is an undiſtinguiſhed Deſtruction, of all Ages, Sexes and Conditions.

In every ſtage of theſe Oppreſſions we have Petitioned for Redreſs in the moſt humble Terms: Our repeated Petitions have been anſwered only by repeated Injury. A Prince, whoſe Character is thus marked by every act which may define a Tyrant, is unfit to be the Ruler of a free People.

Nor have we been wanting in Attentions to our Britiſh Brethren. We have warned them from Time to Time of Attempts by their Legiſlature to extend an unwarrantable Juriſdiction over us. We have reminded them of the Circumſtances of our Emigration and Settlement here. We have appealed to their native Juſtice and Magnanimity, and we have conjured them by the Ties of our common Kindred to diſavow theſe Uſurpations, which, would inevitably interrupt our Connections and Correſpondence. They too have been deaf to the Voice of Juſtice and of Conſanguinity. We muſt, therefore, acquieſce in the Neceſſity, which denounces our Separation, and hold them, as we hold the reſt of Mankind, Enemies in War, in Peace, Friends.

We, therefore, the Repreſentatives of the UNITED STATES OF AMERICA, in GENERAL CONGRESS, Aſſembled, appealing to the Supreme Judge of the World for the Rectitude of our Intentions, do, in the Name, and by Authority of the good People of theſe Colonies, ſolemnly Publiſh and Declare, That theſe United Colonies are, and of Right ought to be, FREE AND INDEPENDENT STATES; that they are abſolved from all Allegiance to the Britiſh Crown, and that all political Connection between them and the State of Great-Britain, is and ought to be totally diſſolved; and that as FREE AND INDEPENDENT STATES, they have full Power to levy War, conclude Peace, contract Alliances, eſtabliſh Commerce, and to do all other Acts and Things which INDEPENDENT STATES may of right do. And for the ſupport of this Declaration, with a firm Reliance on the Protection of divine Providence, we mutually pledge to each other our Lives, our Fortunes, and our ſacred Honor.

Signed by ORDER and in BEHALF of the CONGRESS,

JOHN HANCOCK, PRESIDENT.

ATTEST.
CHARLES THOMSON, SECRETARY.

PHILADELPHIA: PRINTED BY JOHN DUNLAP.

The Declaration of Independence

1776   In the Historical Society collection before 1812.

The first printing of the document that founded the nation is the most important publication in the Historical Society collections. John Dunlap, a Philadelphia newspaper printer, turned out a small number of broadside copies on the night of 4–5 July, and independence was proclaimed in Philadelphia on 5 July 1776. On 18 July, Abigail Adams was in the crowd that heard the Declaration read aloud—perhaps from this very copy—from the balcony of the Old State House in Boston.

John Adams served with Thomas Jefferson, Benjamin Franklin, Roger Sherman, and Robert R. Livingston on the Committee of Five that the Continental Congress appointed to draft the Declaration. Jefferson prepared a rough draft that was revised by Adams and Franklin. Congress voted to adopt a resolution for independence on 2 July and continued to revise the Declaration until 4 July, when it authorized the Committee to print the corrected text.

In the documents that follow, the Declaration of Independence serves as a case study for the use of personal papers—letters and documents written by John and Abigail Adams and Thomas Jefferson—in the study of an epochal event in American history.

the House and Furniture of the Solisiter General have fallen
a prey to their own merciless party— Surely the very fiends
feel a preverential awe for virtuess patriotism, whilst they
Detest the parricide & traitor ———

I feel very differently at the ap
proach of Spring to what I did a month ago, we knew not
then whether we could plant or sow with Safety, whether when
we had toild we could reap the fruits of our own industry, whett
we could rest in our own Cottages, or whether we should not
be driven from the Sea coasts to seek shelter in the wilderness
but now we feel as if we might sit under our own vine
and eat the good of the land— I feel a gaieti de Coar
to which before I was a Stranger, I think the Sun looks
brighter the birds sing more melodiously, & nature puts on
a more chearfull countanance— we feel a temporary
peace, & the poor fugitives are returning to their deserted habitations
                        tho we felicitate ourselves, we sympa
thize with those who are trembling least the Lot of Boston
should be theirs—But they cannot be in similar circumstances
unless pusilanimity & cowardise should take possession of
them— They have time & warning given them to see
the Evil & shun it— I long to hear that you have de
clared an independancy— and by the way in the new
Code of Laws which I suppose it will be necessary for you
to make I desire you would Remember the Ladies, &
be more generous & favourable to them than your ancestors
do not put such unlimited power into the hands of the
Husbands. remember all Men would be tyrants if they
could. if perticuliar care & attention is not paid to the
Laidies we are determined to foment a Rebelion, and will
not hold ourselves bound by any Laws in which we have
no voice, or representation—

Abigail Adams ~ Letter to John Adams

31 MARCH ~ 5 APRIL 1776   Gift of the Adams Manuscript Trust, 1956.

In the spring of 1776, with talk of independence in the air, Abigail Adams famously advised her husband,

> *I long to hear that you have declared an independancy —and by the way in the New Code of Laws which I suppose it will be necessary for you to make I desire you would Remember the Ladies, & be more Generous & favourable to them than your ancestors.*

Eliza Susan Quincy ~ Birthplaces of John Adams and John Quincy Adams, 1822. Gift of Eliza Susan Quincy, 1870.

A Declaration by the Representatives of the United States of America in General Congress assembled.

When in the course of human events it becomes necessary for one people to dissolve the political bands which have connected them with another, & to assume among the powers of the earth the separate & equal station, to which the laws of nature & of nature's god entitle them, a decent respect to the opinions of mankind requires that they should declare the causes which impel them to the separation.

We hold these truths to be self-evident: that all men are created equal: that ~~they are endowed by their creator~~ with inherent & inalienable rights; that ~~a~~ these are life, liberty, & the pursuit of happiness: that to secure these rights, governments are instituted among men, deriving their just powers from the consent of the governed: that whenever any form of government becomes destructive of these ends, it is the right of the people to alter or to abolish it, & to institute new government, laying it's foundation on such principles, & organising it's powers in such form, as to them shall seem most likely to effect their safety and happiness. prudence indeed will dictate that governments long established should not be changed for light and transient causes: and accordingly all experience hath shewn that mankind are more disposed to suffer while evils are sufferable, than to right themselves by abolishing the forms to which they are accustomed. but when a long train of abuses & usurpations, begun at a distinguished period, & pursuing invariably the same object, evinces a design to reduce them under absolute despotism, it is their right, it is their duty, to throw off such government, & to provide new guards for their future security. such has been the patient sufferance of these colonies; and such is now the necessity which constrains them to expunge their former systems of government. the history of the present king of Great Britain is a history of unremitting injuries & usurpations, among which appears no solitary fact to contradict the uniform tenor of the rest, but all have in direct object the establishment of an absolute tyranny over these states. to prove this, let facts be submitted to a candid world, for the truth of which we pledge a faith yet unsullied by falsehood.

He has refused his assent to laws the most wholesome and necessary for the public good.

he has forbidden his governors to pass laws of immediate & pressing importance, unless suspended in their operation till his assent should be obtained; and when so suspended, he has neglected utterly to attend to them.

Thomas Jefferson ~
The Declaration of Independence

1776 Manuscript copy. Gift of Mr. and Mrs. Alexander C. Washburn, 1893.

Jefferson's draft of the Declaration was subjected to considerable Congressional revision. He was extremely unhappy with many of the changes and made several copies of the Declaration "as originally framed," including this one, to show his close friends how his text had been "mangled."

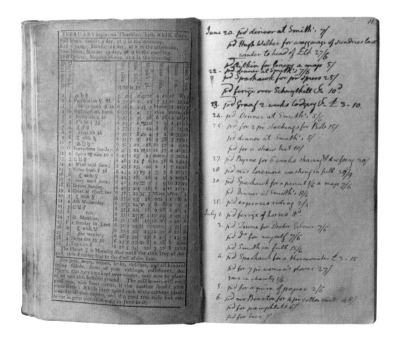

Thomas Jefferson ~ Memorandum book, 1776–1778.
Gift of Thomas Jefferson Coolidge, 1898.

Jefferson did not realize 4 July 1776 would become the "day of days." On that date, he recorded in his pocket account book shopping for a thermometer and gloves.

Philadelphia July 3.d 1776

Had a Declaration of Independency been made
Seven Months ago, it would have been attended with many great and
glorious Effects. ~ ~ ~ We might before this Hour, have formed
Alliances with foreign States. — We should have mastered Quebec
and been in Possession of Canada. ~ ~ ~ You will perhaps
wonder, how Such a Declaration would have influenced our
Affairs, in Canada, but if I could write with Freedom I could
easily convince you, that it would, and explain to you the
manner how. ~ The Many Gentlemen in high Stations and
of great Influence have been duped, by the ministerial Bubble
of Commissioners to treat. ~ ~ ~ and in real, Sincere Expecta
tion of this Event, while they so fondly wished, they have been Slow
and languid in promoting Measures for the Reduction of that
Province. Others there are who really wished that our Enter
prise in Canada would be defeated, that the Colonies might
be brought into Danger and Distress between two Fires, and
be thus induced to Submit. ~ ~ Others, really wished to defeat
the Expedition to Canada, lest the Conquest of it, should elevate
the Minds of the People too much to hearken to those Terms
of Reconciliation which they believed would be offered Us.
These jarring Views and Designs, occasioned an opposition to many
Salutary Measures, which were proposed for the Support of that
Expedition, and caused Obstructions, Embarrassments and fruitless
Delays, which have finally, lost Us the Province.

John Adams ~ Letter to Abigail Adams

3 JULY 1776   Gift of the Adams Manuscript Trust, 1956.

John Adams seems to have understood more clearly than any other member of the Continental Congress the momentous importance of the vote for independence and how it would be celebrated by "succeeding Generations." He was right about everything except the date:

> *The Second Day of July 1776, will be the most memorable Epocha, in the History of America.— I am apt to believe that it will be celebrated, by succeeding Generations, as the great anniversary Festival. It ought to be commemorated, as the Day of Deliverance by Solemn Acts of Devotion to God Almighty. It ought to be Solemnized with Pomp and Parade with Shews, Games, Sports, Guns, Bells, Bonfires and Illuminations from one End of this Continent to the other from this Time forward forever more.*

All these Causes however in Conjunction would not have disappointed Us, if it had not been for a Misfortune, which could not be fore seen, and perhaps could not have been prevented, I mean the Prevalence of the Small Pox among our Troops. ᴀ ᴀ ᴀ This fatal Pestilence, compleated our Destruction.— It is a Frown of Providence upon Us, which We ought to lay to heart.—

But on the other Hand, the Delay of this Declaration to this Time, has many great Advantages attending it.— The Hopes of Reconciliation, which were fondly entertained by Multitudes of honest and well meaning tho weak and mistaken People, have been gradually and at last totally extinguished.— Time has been given for the whole People, maturely to consider the great Question of Independence and to ripen their Judgment, dissipate their Fears and allure their Hopes, by discussing it in News Papers and Pamphlets, by debating it, in Assemblies, Conventions, Committees of Safety and Inspection in Town and County Meetings, as well as in private conversations, so that the whole People in every Colony of the 13, have now adopted it, as their own Act.— This will cement the Union, and avoid those Heats and perhaps Convulsions which might have been occasioned, by such a Declaration Six Months ago.—

But the Day is past.— The Second Day of July 1776, will be the most memorable Epocha, in the History of America.—

I am apt to believe that it will be celebrated, by succeeding Generations, as the great anniversary Festival. It ought to be commemorated, as the Day of Deliverance by solemn Acts of Devotion to God Almighty. It ought to be solemnized with Pomp and Parade with shews, Games, Sports, Guns, Bells, Bonfires and Illuminations from one End of this Continent to the other from this Time forward forever more.

You will think me transported with Enthusiasm but I am not. — I am well aware of the Toil and Blood and Treasure, that it will cost Us to maintain this Declaration, and support and defend these States. — Yet through all the Gloom I can see the Rays of ravishing Light and Glory. I can see that the End is more than worth all the Means. And that Posterity will tryumph in that Days Transaction, even altho We should rue it, which I trust in God We shall not. —

Dear Sir   Monticello Mar. 25.26.

My grandson Th:Jefferson Randolph, being on a visit to Boston, would think he had seen nothing were he to leave it without having seen you. altho' I truly sympathise with you in the trouble these interruptions give, yet I must ask for him permission to pay to you his personal respects. like other young people, he wishes to be able, in the winter nights of old age, to recount to those around him what he has heard and learnt of the Heroic age preceding his birth, and which of the Argonauts particularly he was in time to have seen. it was the lot of our early years to witness nothing but the dull monotony of colonial subservience, and of our riper ones to breast the labors and perils of working out of it. theirs are the Halcyon calms succeeding the storm which our Argosy had so stoutly weathered. gratify his ambition then by recieving his best bow, and my solicitude for your health by enabling him to bring me a favorable account of it. mine is but indifferent, but not so my friendship and respect for you.

Th:Jefferson

Thomas Jefferson ~ Letter to John Adams

25 MARCH 1826   Gift of the Adams Manuscript Trust, 1956.

The story of the friendship of John Adams and Thomas Jefferson, completely broken in the aftermath of the bitter presidential election campaign of 1800, has a happy ending. Through the intervention of their mutual friend Dr. Benjamin Rush, Adams and Jefferson resumed their correspondence after a decade of silence. Over the next fourteen years (1812–1826), hundreds of letters flowed back and forth between Quincy and Monticello. In Thomas Jefferson's last letter to John Adams, he compares their roles in the Revolution to those of the Argonauts of Greek mythology: "It was the lot of our early years to witness nothing but the dull monotony of Colonial subservience, and of our riper ones to breast the labors and perils of working out of it."

While this letter from Jefferson to Adams is located in the Adams Family Papers, the Historical Society also holds an extraordinary collection of Jefferson's personal papers, the Coolidge Collection of Thomas Jefferson Manuscripts. The Coolidge Collection includes thousands of letters to Jefferson and copies of his replies, together with hundreds of his architectural drawings, the manuscript catalog of his library, and the farm and garden records of Monticello.

Meridian Hill 25 March 1829.

Louisa C. Adams.

John Q. Adams.

John Adams

Mary L. Adams

Mary C. Adams

Abigail B. Adams

Mary Roberdeau

Jarvis F. Hanks ~
The Family of John Quincy Adams

25 MARCH 1829   Gift of Richard Ames, 2002.

John Quincy Adams's single term as president was the unhappiest period of his long career in public service. Badly defeated in his bid for re-election in 1830, there was a brief hiatus in Adams's political career before he returned to office, serving as a member of Congress from 1830 until his death in 1848. Shortly after the Adams family left the White House for their home on Meridian Hill, John Quincy Adams noted in his diary,

> *Mr. Reynolds came with master Hankes who cut me out and all the family in paper. I had my wife and myself; my son John, his wife and their baby [Mary C. Adams and Mary L. Adams], Mary Roberdeau [daughter of family friend Isaac Roberdeau, of Philadelphia] and Abigail S. Adams [his niece, daughter of his brother, Thomas Boylston Adams], all cut out and pasted upon one Card.*

All are neatly labeled in John Quincy Adams's own hand.

The FRIGHTE[?]
of 10 6 Poun[?]

The HORRE[?]
of 8 6 Pounder[?]

John Quincy Adams ~ Illustrations from the end papers of volume 2 of his diary

1780   Gift of the Adams Manuscript Trust, 1956.

John Quincy Adams began to keep a diary when he sailed with his father to France in 1779, a diary that became over the course of sixty-eight years one of the most remarkable documents in American history—truly an American treasure.

following pages

John Quincy Adams ~ Diary entry

29 MARCH 1841   Gift of the Adams Manuscript Trust, 1956.

In his seventy-fourth year, John Quincy Adams appeared before the United States Supreme Court to argue on behalf of Africans who had been kidnapped into slavery in Cuba but who had escaped to the United States by capturing the ship on which they were held, the *Amistad*.

Washington, Monday 29. March 1841.   Fire

Rain the greater part of the last night, and of this day, with a chilling east wind requiring a small fire in my chamber; just enough to be kept burning

Mr. Munroe was a stranger from Boston, who brought a parcel for Elizabeth. I completed the assortment and filing of my Letters received since the beginning of this year, and find myself with a task before me perfectly appalling. I am yet to revise for publication my argument in the case of the Amistad Africans, and in merely glancing over the Parliamentary Slave trade papers lent me by Mr. Fox, I find impulses of duty upon my own conscience which I cannot resist, while on the other hand, the magnitude, the danger, the insurmountable burden of labour to be encountered in the undertaking to touch upon the Slave-trade. No one else will undertake it. No one but a spirit unconquerable by man Woman or Friend, can undertake it, but with the help of martyrdom. The world, the flesh, and all the devils in hell are arrayed against any man, who now, in this North-American Union shall dare to join the standard of Almighty God, to put down the African Slave-trade. and what can I, upon the verge of my seventy. fourth birthday, with a shaking hand, a darkening eye, a drowsy brain, and with all my faculties dropping from me, one by one, as the teeth are dropping from my head, one by one, what can I do for the cause of God and man? for the progress of human emancipation? for the suppression of the African Slave trade? Yet my conscience presses me on — Let me but die upon the breach ——— I walked about half an hour for exercise before dinner, and called at the house of Mr. S. H. Fox the British Minister to have some conversation with him. It was 2. o'clock & the Servant at the door told me that he was not up, and that he was unwell. I enquired at what time he was usually visible. he said between 3. and 4. I had heard that his usual hour of rising was 3. In my second walk after dinner I met Mr. Jesse D. Miller, first Auditor of the Treasury; from which office it is said he is to retire at the close of the present month and quarter. This evening I answered an old and repeated invitation to deliver a Lecture at Richmond Virginia; and postponed answering the Letters received last Evening from the Amistad Committee, and from Lewis Tappan. I read Judge Betts's opinion upon the 14th Section of the Tariff Act of July 1832. and the reversal of his decision by Judge Thompson. And I made several minutes from the Parliamentary Slave trade papers Class A. 1839. 40. shewing the enormous extent to which that trade was in those and the two preceding years, carried on in American Vessels under the patronage of N. P. Trist.

Washington Tuesday 30. March 1841.   Alexandria.

IV: 45. Tuesday.
Gordon Charles
Hallowell Benjamin
Janney Phineas
Homer James Lloyd
Allen Walter
Thomas James.

Mr Charles Gordon heretofore an important clerk
in the General Land Office dismissed under the
Jackson administration for the colour of his political
coat, afterwards employed three several times by
direction of the Senate as a draughtsman to protract
the Lands Surveys came to shew me a machine of his
own invention for protracting surveys made by the chain
and compass. His dismission according to his statement was one of the first steps
that chaos of confusion into which the whole management of the Office has
fallen, the extent of which may be imagined from the necessity of an act of Congress actually passed at the recent Session to legalize the whole mass of the
land Patents issued for several years. Mr Gordon want restoration to his
place. Mr Homer came to set forth his equitable claims to a clerkship in one of
the Departments here, consisting 1. In his wants 2. In his misfortunes, having
failed in business as publisher of a compound newspaper in Boston 3. In the fact
that there is not a single Boston man in any of the subordinate public offices.
His purpose is to be a letter writer for sundry Newspapers; for which a Clerkship will be a convenient location. He had a recommendation signed by
Mr Choate and some others, but Mr Bates had neglected him; and it was said
the members of the Massachusetts were not so zealous in supporting the appli-
cations of their constituents for office as others, but Mr Webster had advised him
to apply to Mr Ewing and Mr Granger, whose Departments had much more
patronage than his, but said that if he should fail with them, after all, he
would take care of him. He promised to send me a copy of his address to the
Boston Charitable Mechanic Association in 1836. Col° James Thomas was
here and gave me many details of the competitions for Office and for the
removal of Office some of which are humiliating. Walter S. Allen likewise
called. Mr Hallowell and Mr Janney came with a carriage from Alexandria and took me down there, where I dined with Mr Edmund Jennings Lee
and a party of ten of his family and friends among whom were Mr I. Fowle,
lately the Episcopalian Minister of the Church, his son Cassius Lee with his
wife a married daughter, besides Mrs Lee Hallowell, Janney and two or three
others. After dinner, with most of the same company and some others, we took
tea at Benjamin Hallowell's - then at half past seven we went to the Lyceum
where I delivered my Lecture on Society and civilization to a crowded audience, after which there was a debate on the question whether phrenology is
a science useful to the community. The meeting broke up between 9 and
10 and I returned with Mr Lee to lodge at his house.

POLITICS & WAR

Beloued Sr

I thanke you for your leter touching mrs Huchingson. I heard since
of a monsterous, & prodigious birth which she should discouer amongst
you, as also that she should retracte her confession or aknow=
lodgmente of those errours, before she wente away; of which I
haue heard many various reports. If your leasure would per=
mite, I should be much beholden unto you, to sertifie me in a word
or tow, of y truck & forme of y monster &c.   vpon y ynformation
& complainte of our neigbours at sityate, I am requested by our
assistants to write unto you, touching a late partition, or limiting
of confines, betweene you & vs; of which we heard noking till of
late. Wherin we vnderstande you haue yntrenched farr vpon
those lands, which we haue conceiued to belong to vs by right diuers
waies; as first by composission & compacte with y natiues to whom y
right & souerainite of them did belonge, which did extend as farr
as conazasete, which was y bounds betweene y sachimos of y massa=
chusets, & those of these parts; 2ly It since hath been confirmed vnto vs
by patente from his majesties authoritie. 3ly heronon we haue
posest it, & planted it some years agoe. We desire you will giue
vs a reason of your proceedings herin; as also that that ther may
be a faire, & freindly desission of y controuercie; that we may pre=
serue peace & brotherly loue amongst our selues, that haue so many
enimies abroad.   ther was not long since here with vs in colling=
ton & some other of your people, who brought mr williams with them
and prest vs hard for a place at, or near sowamos, the which
we denid them; then mr williams ynformed them of a seuerations
yland caled monachunte, touching which I solisited our good
will, to which we yeelded (so they would compound with y same quinte)
y which we heard was yll taken by you, but you may please to vnder
stand y it is not yn our patente (though we tould them not so) for
It only was excepted out of it.) And we thought (yf they liked it)
It were better to haue them, (though they differ in oppinions) then
(easily) worse neigbours, both for vs, & you. We thinke it is also
better for vs both to haue some strength in y bay. thus comend=
ing you, & your afaires to y Lord, with my loue remembred to your
selfe, & the rest of my worthy friends with you, I take leaue &
rest

Aprill. 11.
1638   your vnworthy freind
                                                william Bradford

William Bradford ~ Letter to John Winthrop

11 APRIL 1638   Bequest of Robert C. Winthrop, Jr., 1905.

Governor William Bradford of Plymouth Colony writes to
Governor John Winthrop of the Massachusetts Bay Colony
about Anne Hutchinson ("Mrs. Huchinson"), who soon would be
exiled from Massachusetts Bay in the aftermath of the Antino-
mian Controversy, and her supporter Mary Dyer, who would die
as a martyr to religious freedom in 1660.

Winthrop family flint pouch with striking iron, 17th century.
Bequest of Clara Bowdoin Winthrop, 1969.

A PARTICULAR PLAN

OF

LAKE GEORGE.

Surveyed in 1756.

By CAP.ᵗ JACKSON.

Scale of Miles.

Observations.

Lake George which was called by the French Lac du S.ᵗ Sacrement
is named by the Indians Caniad-eri-oit, that is, Tail of the Lake.
It is bounded on both Sides with exceeding high Mountains: Its
Navigation is obstructed, at the Northern End, by a Ridge of Rocks
over which the Surplus Issue of its Waters Falls.
The Course which our Troops took during the Last War was
generally to Land on Sabbath Day Point, whence a
Road Leads to Ticonderago.

* Topog. Descrip. p.18.
by Gov.ʳ Townall.

French Point

Sabbath Day Point

Point Pleasant

A. Fort William Henry, afterwards Fort George.
B. Bridge.
C. Lime Kilns.
D. Brick-Yard.
E. A Rising Ground that overlooks the Fort.
✗ Where S.ʳ W.ᵐ Johnson, defeated Gen.ˡ Dieskau Sep.ᵗ 8.ᵗ 1755.
NB. The Figures denote Fathoms.

Otter Creek

This Road was opened by the New
Hampshire Province during the War

....ller N.º 53 Fleet Street. as the Act directs. Aug.ᵗ 5.ᵗ 1776.

William Brassier ~ Inset map of A Survey of Lake Champlain including Lake George

1776 From Atlas des Colonies Angloises en Amérique.
Gift of Count Jules de Menou, 1859.

The Lake Champlain–Lake George corridor was a prime invasion route for armies during the French and Indian War, the American Revolution, and the War of 1812. At the southern end of Lake Champlain a short portage connects to Lake George, which in turn connects via a twelve-mile portage to the Hudson River.

Gentlemen,

By an anonymous sum=
mons, an attempt has been made to con
vene you together ____ how inconsis
tent with the rules of propriety! ___
how unmilitary! ___ and how sub=
versive of all order and discipline
.___ let the good sense of the Army
decide.___

In the moment of this sum
mons, another anonymous product=
on was sent into circulation; ad
dressed more to the feelings & passi
ons, than to the reason & judgment
of the Army. ___ The Author of the
piece, is entitled to much credit for
the goodness of his Pen:___ and I could
wish he had as much credit for the
rectitude of his Heart___ for, as men
see thro' different Optics, and are
induced by the reflecting faculties
of the Mind, to use different means
to attain the same end; ___ the Autho
of the Address, should have had
more charity, than to mark for

George Washington ~ Newburgh Address

15 MARCH 1783   Gift of William A. Hayes, 1821.

At Newburgh, New York, during the waning days of the
Revolution, George Washington confronted one of the greatest
challenges to his command. The disgruntled officers of the
Continental Army, long unpaid, threatened to force Congress
to meet their demands. Washington's eloquent address to his
officers recalled them to their duty and quelled their agitation
before it became an open revolt. He appealed to both their military honor and their sentimental attachment to him. Having
"grown gray" in their shared service, Washington found that he
was "growing blind" and could not read his own handwritten
address without stopping to put on his spectacles.

Pierre Simon Benjamin Duvivier, engraver ~ Washington before Boston medal,
1785–1789. Gift of Peter Harvey, 1874.

Congress awarded Washington this medal for his "wise and spirited conduct in the
siege and acquisition of Boston."

WE the People of the States of New-Hampshire, Massachusetts, Rhode-Island and Providence Plantations, Connecticut, New-York, New-Jersey, Pennsylvania, Delaware, Maryland, Virginia, North-Carolina, South-Carolina, and Georgia, do ordain, declare and establish the following Constitution for the Government of Ourselves and our Posterity.

ARTICLE I.

The stile of this Government shall be, " The United States of America."

II.

The Government shall consist of supreme legislative, executive and judicial powers.

III.

The legislative power shall be vested in a Congress, to consist of two separate and distinct bodies of men, a House of Representatives, and a Senate ; ~~each of which shall, in all cases, have a negative on the other.~~ The Legislature shall meet on the first Monday in December ~~in every year.~~

IV.

Sect. 1. The Members of the House of Representatives shall be chosen every second year, by the people of the several States comprehended within this Union. The qualifications of the electors shall be the same, from time to time, as those of the electors in the several States, of the most numerous branch of their own legislatures.

Sect. 2. Every Member of the House of Representatives shall be of the age of twenty-five years at least; shall have been a citizen in the United States for at least ~~three~~ years before his election, and shall be, at the time of his election, ~~a resident~~ of the State in which he shall be chosen.

Sect. 3. The House of Representatives shall, at its first formation, and until the number of citizens and inhabitants shall be taken in the manner herein after described, consist of sixty-five Members, of whom three shall be chosen in New-Hampshire, eight in Massachusetts, one in Rhode-Island and Providence Plantations, five in Connecticut, six in New-York, four in New-Jersey, eight in Pennsylvania, one in Delaware, six in Maryland, ten in Virginia, five in North-Carolina, five in South-Carolina, and three in Georgia.

Sect. 4. As the proportions of numbers in the different States will alter from time to time; as some of the States may hereafter be divided; as others may be enlarged by addition of territory; as two or more States may be united; as new States will be erected within the limits of the United States, the Legislature shall, in each of these cases, regulate the number of representatives by the number of inhabitants, according to the ~~provisions herein after made,~~ at the rate of one for every forty thousand.

Sect. 5. All bills for raising or appropriating money, and for fixing the salaries of the officers of government, shall originate in the House of Representatives, and shall not be altered or amended by the Senate. No money shall be drawn from the public Treasury, but in pursuance of appropriations that shall originate in the House of Representatives.

Sect. 6. The House of Representatives shall have the sole power of impeachment. It shall choose its Speaker and other officers.

Sect. 7. Vacancies in the House of Representatives shall be supplied by writs of election from the executive authority of the State, in the representation from which they shall happen.

V.

United States Constitution

6 AUGUST 1787   Gift of James T. Austin, 1829.

Elbridge Gerry's annotated copy of the first printed draft of the
United States Constitution shows the evolution of the text as it
was amended during the debates in the Philadelphia Convention
of 1787. Gerry, a delegate from Massachusetts and signer of the
Declaration of Independence, followed the debates carefully but
refused to sign the Constitution because it contained no Bill of
Rights. He later served in Congress, was governor of Massachusetts, and was vice president of the United States at the time of
his death in 1814.

Susan Anne Livingston Ridley Sedgwick ~ Portrait of Elizabeth Freeman

1811   Gift of Maria Banyer Sedgwick, 1884.

Elizabeth Freeman, familiarly known as "Mumbet," sued for her freedom from Colonel John Ashley of Sheffield, Massachusetts, in 1783, setting the legal precedent for the abolition of slavery in Massachusetts. She was represented by Theodore Sedgwick, who argued that Freeman should be freed under the Bill of Rights of the Massachusetts Constitution. It reads, "all men are born free and equal, and have certain natural, essential, and inalienable rights." Mumbet gave the necklace that she wears in this portrait to Theodore Sedgwick's daughter, the novelist Catharine Maria Sedgwick, who made them into a double strand bracelet.

Bracelet made from beads of a necklace worn by Elizabeth Freeman, circa 1840. Gift of William Minot, 1884.

NO SLAVERY!

FOURTH OF JULY!

The Managers of the

Mass. ANTI-SLAVERY SOC'Y

Invite, without distinction of party or sect, ALL who are ready and mean to be known as on LIBER-TY'S side, in the great struggle which is now upon us, to meet in convention at the

GROVE IN FRAMINGHAM,

On the approaching FOURTH OF JULY, there to pass the day in no idle glorying in our country's liberties, but in deep humiliation for her Disgrace and Shame, and in resolute purpose---God being our leader--- to rescue old Massachusetts at least from being bound forever to the car of Slavery.

SPECIAL TRAINS

Will be run on that day, TO THE GROVE, from Boston, Worcester, and Milford, leaving each place at 9 25 A. M.

RETURNING---Leave the Grove about 5 1-2 P. M. FARE, by all these Trains, to the Grove and back,

FIFTY CENTS.

The beauty of the Grove, and the completeness and excellence of its accommodations, are well known.

EMINENT SPEAKERS,

From different quarters of the State, will be present.

Earle & Drew, Printers, 212 Main Street, Worcester.

No Slavery ~ Fourth of July

1854   From the Historical Society broadside collection.

In 1854, the Massachusetts Anti-Slavery Society sponsored a Fourth of July rally in Framingham, where noted abolitionists including William Lloyd Garrison, Sojourner Truth, and Henry David Thoreau addressed the crowd. At the climax of the meeting, Garrison burned copies of the 1850 Fugitive Slave Law and the United States Constitution, proclaiming the Constitution "a covenant with death and an agreement with hell."

following pages

The Branded Hand

1845   Albert S. Southworth and Josiah J. Hawes.
Gift of Nathaniel Bowditch, 1930.

In 1844, the letters "S.S."—for slave stealer—were branded on the right hand (the image is reversed in this early photograph) of Captain Jonathan Walker, a Cape Cod ship captain and ardent abolitionist who was arrested during a failed attempt to sail escaped slaves from Florida to the West Indies.

Rec. 21 Nov. 1863.

Executive Mansion,

Washington, Nov. 20 , 1863 .

Hon. Edward Everett.

My dear Sir:

Your kind note of to-day is received. In our respective parts yesterday, you could not have been excused to make a short address, nor I a long one. I am pleased to know that, in your judgment, the little I did say was not entirely a failure— Of course I knew Mr Everett would not fail; and yet, while the whole discourse was eminently satisfactory, and will be of great value, there were passages in it which transcended my expectation. The point made against the theory of the general government being only an agency, whose principals are the States, was new to me, and, as I think, is one of the best arguments for the national supremacy. The tribute to our noble women for their angel-ministering to the suffering soldiers, surpasses, in its way, as do the subjects of it, whatever has gone before—

Our sick boy, for whom you kindly inquire, we hope is past the worst,

Your Obt. Servt.
A. Lincoln

Abraham Lincoln ~ Letter to Edward Everett

20 NOVEMBER 1863   Gift of the heirs of Edward Everett, 1930.

On 19 November 1863, the national cemetery was dedicated at Gettysburg. Edward Everett of Massachusetts, the greatest orator of the day, was the primary speaker. The next day, Everett and Lincoln exchanged letters concerning their respective roles in the ceremony. Everett wrote to Lincoln,

> *I should be glad, if I could flatter myself, that I came as near to the central idea of the occasion in two hours as you did in two minutes.*

Lincoln replied the same day,

> *In our respective parts yesterday, you could not have been excused to make a short address, nor I a long one. I am pleased to know that, in your judgment, the little I did say was not entirely a failure.*

Abraham Lincoln / Andrew Johnson presidential campaign token, 1864.
Anonymous gift in the late 19th or early 20th century.

Sergeant Henry Steward

1863 Unidentified photographer. Gift of Mary Silsbee Emilio, 1920.

After President Lincoln issued the Emancipation Proclamation in December 1862, Massachusetts was the first state to respond by enlisting African American soldiers. The Historical Society holds many manuscripts and photographs that document the service of Black soldiers and sailors in the Civil War. Highlights include those found in the personal papers of Governor John A. Andrew, who ordered the recruitment of the Massachusetts Fifty-Fourth Volunteer Infantry Regiment and offered the command to Robert Gould Shaw, as well as photographs and other materials collected for a history of the regiment by the commander of Company E, Captain Luis Fenollosa Emilio.

Sergeant Henry Steward (or Stewart) was a 23-year-old farmer from Adrian, Michigan, who enlisted in Emilio's company of the Fifty-Fourth Regiment on 4 April 1863. Steward died of disease at Morris Island, South Carolina, on 27 September of that year.

To surrender & render outside
have heavy
reinforcements   Santiago.
sent us
instantly. July 3ᵈ 98

Dear Cabot;

              Tell the
President for heaven's
sake to send us
every regiment and
above all every battery
possible. We have
won so far, al—

We could in many ways with honor
Allof I may—

Theodore Roosevelt ~ Letter to Henry Cabot Lodge

3 JULY 1898   Gift of Henry Cabot Lodge, Jr., 1969.

Tell the President for Heavens sake to send us every regiment and above all every battery possible.

Writing from the trenches outside of Santiago, Cuba, just after the Battle of San Juan Hill, Theodore Roosevelt thought that the campaign in Cuba—the event that was to make his political career—appeared to be on the verge of catastrophe. Within a few months of writing this letter, Roosevelt would be elected governor of New York.

Theodore Roosevelt in his Rough Rider uniform, 1898.
Photograph by Rockwood. Gift of Henry Cabot Lodge, Jr., 1969.

Joan of Arc Saved France

WOMEN OF AMERICA
SAVE YOUR COUNTRY
Buy WAR SAVINGS STAMPS

UNITED STATES TREASURY DEPARTMENT

Haskell Coffin ~ Joan of Arc Saved France

1918   Gift of Henry Cabot Lodge, 1918.

More than 20,000 American women answered the call during the First World War, serving in the armed forces or as Red Cross and YWCA volunteers.

Margaret Hall

11 NOVEMBER 1918   Photograph used to illustrate an entry in her Letters and Photographs from the Battle Country, 1918–1919. Gift of Emma L. Coleman, 1927.

Margaret Hall compiled a typescript narrative from letters and diary passages written while she was a member of the American Red Cross in France during World War I, and she copiously illustrated it with her own photographs.

August 5, 1963

Dear Senator Saltonstall:

I am returning your letter from Mr. Bradley in which we are informed that there are some in Ireland who think you are my uncle. If you are ready to admit it, I am.

With best wishes.

Sincerely,

The Honorable
   Leverett Saltonstall
   United States Senate
   Washington, D. C.

John F. Kennedy ~ Letter to Leverett Saltonstall

5 AUGUST 1963   Gift of Leverett Saltonstall, 1967.

Senator Leverett Saltonstall heard through a friend, Ralph
Bradley, that Philip Hofer, during a visit to Ireland in 1963, had
been asked by a local man about the health of "That old Senator
Saltonstall—him, that is uncle to Pres. Kennedy." Saltonstall sent
the story on to the president, who replied, "we are informed that
there are some in Ireland who think you are my uncle. If you are
ready to admit it, I am."

John F. Kennedy and Leverett Saltonstall, by an unknown photographer, 1959.
Gift of Leverett Saltonstall, 1967.

MATHEMATICS & PHILOSOPHY
NAVIGATION & COMMERCE

MAMUSSE
WUNNEETUPANATAMWE
UP-BIBLUM GOD
NANEESWE
NUKKONE TESTAMENT
KAH WONK
WUSKU TESTAMENT.

Ne quoſhkinnumuk naſhpe Wuttinneumoh *CHRIST*
noh aſcoweſit

JOHN ELIOT.

CAMBRIDGE:

Printeuoop naſhpe *Samuel Green* kah *Marmaduke Johnſon.*

1663.

Mamusse Wunneetupanatamwe Up-Biblum God ~ The Eliot Indian Bible

1663   Gift of a Mrs. Coffin, 1793.

According to the Charter of the Massachusetts Bay Company, "the principall ende of this plantation . . . [is] to wyn and incite the natives of the country, to the knowledge and obedience of the onlie true God." Reverend John Eliot, the chief missionary agent in this effort, undertook to translate and publish the Bible in the Algonquin language spoken in eastern New England. The "Eliot Indian Bible" was the first large-scale printing project in Massachusetts. In the end, however, it was a tragic failure; most copies were destroyed in the turmoil of King Philip's War, which was, per capita, the most destructive war in American history.

following pages

John Foster ~ A Map of New England

1677   Gift of Robert C. Winthrop, Jr., 1895.

The first map engraved and printed in British North America is attributed to John Foster, a mathematician and schoolmaster, who was the first printer in Boston. The map originally appeared in William Hubbard's *A Narrative of the Troubles with the Indians in New-England,* the best early account of the Indian Wars published in America.

There are more than 5,000 historical maps and charts in the Society's collections as well as early printed books illustrated with maps.

A MAP OF
NEW·ENGLAND,

Being the first that ever was here cut, and done by the best Pattern that could be had, which being in some places defective, it made the other less exact: yet doth it sufficiently shew the Scituation of the Country, and conveniently well the distance of Places.

The figures that are joyned with the Names of Places are to distinguish such as have been assaulted by the Indians from others.

A Scale of forty Miles.

10   20   30   4

Deerfield

Squaheag
II

The White Hills

Haveril
37

Rowly
Newbury
Salisbury
Ipswich
Hampton
Dover
Piscatequa R.
42
47   50
Winter-Harbor
51   52

54 55
40
Casco Bay
Kenebeck R.
48

Pemaquid

These may certify, that _Ifrael Keith Efq_ has diligently attended an entire course of my Anatomical Lectures & Demonstrations; together with Physiological & Surgical observations, at the diffecting Theatre in the American Hospital, Boston: whereby he has had an opportunity of acquiring an accurate knowledge in the structure of the human body. _John Warren F.M.S._

BOSTON
March 1e
1782.

Paul Revere ~ Engraver

28 March 1782   Certificate of attendance at Dr. Warren's course of anatomical lectures. Completed in manuscript by John Warren. Gift of Dr. J. Collins Warren, 1921.

Dr. John Warren was the younger brother of Dr. Joseph Warren, the patriot leader who was killed at the Battle of Bunker Hill. During the Revolution, John Warren was the medical director of the military hospital in Boston where he began his anatomical lectures in 1780. He later was a founder of the Harvard Medical School and the Boston Medical Society. The Historical Society's collection of the personal papers of physicians includes four generations of the Warren family.

following pages

Harvard Hall

CIRCA 1700–1750   Embroidery attributed to Mary Leverett Denison Rogers. Given circa 1795.

Samuel Eliot Morison attributed this early embroidered view of Harvard Hall at Harvard College to Mary Leverett, the daughter and granddaughter of Harvard presidents. The Latin motto found on the embroidery is from Virgil. It reads, "They keep out drones from these premises."

The Historical Society holds important collections for the history of education in Massachusetts and has published *Biographical Sketches of Graduates of Harvard University* ("Sibley's Harvard Graduates") since 1873.

Josiah Wolcott ~ Brook Farm with Rainbow

CIRCA 1845   Gift of Mrs. Robert B. Watson, 2005.

In 1841, George and Sophia Ripley founded the Brook Farm
Institute of Agriculture and Education, the best-known utopian
experiment in America, in West Roxbury, Massachusetts. They
envisioned the cooperative community as a social application of
Transcendentalism. To support their experiment in "plain living
and high thinking," the Brook Farmers ran a progressive school;
published a journal devoted to social reform, *The Harbinger;*
and manufactured oil lamps and other utilitarian pewter ware.
In addition to the manuscripts of participants, the Historical
Society holds two contemporary views of Brook Farm painted by
Josiah Wolcott, who was a member of the community.

Pewter oil lamp attributed to Ephraim Capen, Brook Farm, circa 1845–1847.
Gift of Ron Bourgeault, 2006.

The Voyage of the Columbia

At the close of the Revolution, New England merchants were
eager to trade with the East Indies and with Canton, China, in
particular. The ship *Columbia-Rediviva* and the sloop *Lady
Washington* opened the Boston–China Trade by sailing around
Cape Horn to the Northwest coast (hence the name of the
Columbia River) where they traded for sea otter furs, highly
prized in China; on to the Hawaiian Islands for sandalwood;
and then to Canton. During the course of the voyage, the crews
of the *Columbia* and *Lady Washington* distributed copies of
a medal struck to commemorate the "adventure on the Pacific
Ocean." The sponsors also sent a copy to the recently founded
Massachusetts Historical Society. When the *Columbia* returned
to Boston by sailing across the Indian Ocean and around the
Cape of Good Hope, it was the first American ship to circum-
navigate the globe.

Columbia and Washington Medal

1797   Gift of Joseph Barrell on behalf of the merchants who sponsored that voyage.

following pages

Robert Haswell

1787–1789   A Voyage Round the World Onboard the Ship Columbia-Rediviva and
Sloop Washington. Gift of Rebecca Haswell Clarke Cummings, 1947.

A VOYAGE

ROUND THE WORLD

ONBOARD THE SHIP

COLUMBIA-REDIVIVA

and Sloop

WASHINGTON.

A, VOYAGE

ROUND the WORLD

Early in the fitting of the Columbia 1787.
for a Voyage round the World. I was employed Sept.
as a Third Officer; Great expedition was used
to forward our departure and on the
the Ship was hauled off from the wharf and
anchored in the Harbour; here numberless
articles of her provisions stores &c.ᵃ were received
onboard and on the   the pilot came onboard
and we were removed down to the Castle roads
where we anchored with the small bower and
moved with the stream anchor

Friday the   the Sloop Washington
Captain Robt Gray. who is to be our con-
=sort, anchored in the Roads.

Saturday ye   I took my Baggage
onboard and in the afternoon Mr. Ingraham
the second Mate came onboard with his
bagage &c.ᵃ for the first time: till late
in the evening all hands were employed
                              clearing

Paul Revere ~ Urn

CIRCA 1800   Gift of Helen Ford Bradford and Sarah Bradford Ross, 1933.
Photograph © 2009 Museum of Fine Arts, Boston.

To Perpetuate *The Gallant defence* Made by
Captain Gamaliel Bradford *in the Ship Industry
on the 8th of July 1800.*

Gamaliel Bradford received this silver urn for his role in a
dramatic action against French privateers in the Mediterranean
during the undeclared war between the United States and
revolutionary France. A veteran of the American Revolution,
Bradford was an early member of the Historical Society. He lost
a leg in the fight with the privateers but later returned to sea
before retiring to become the warden of the Massachusetts
State Prison.

After the Revolution, Paul Revere continued to work as a gold-
and silversmith, designing pieces in the neoclassical style, but
the Revere family business papers show him to be also a
technological innovator and business entrepreneur. In his
workshops in Boston and Canton, Massachusetts, he began to
produce copper fittings for ships and buildings and cast bells
and cannon.

PAINTING, POETRY, & ARCHITECTURE

John Singleton Copley ~ Portrait of John Hancock

CIRCA 1770–1772   Bequest of Henry Lee Shattuck, 1971.

John Singleton Copley learned to paint and engrave in the
shop of his stepfather, Henry Pelham. Between 1753, the year
of Copley's first works, and 1774, the year he left America for
London, he became eighteenth-century Boston's preeminent
portrait painter. Copley painted this portrait of Hancock soon
after the 1768 seizure of one of his ships, the *Liberty*. The riot
that followed transformed the wealthy Boston merchant into
a patriotic victim of English oppression.

Though portraits were not on its stated lists of preferred collections in its early circular letters, the Historical Society stressed
its desire to be of "public utility," promising to "plant a forest,
into which every inquirer may enter at his pleasure, and find
something adapted to his purpose." The first portrait added to
the collections was an anonymous "head" of Governor Thomas
Hutchinson, traded for a collection of seashells in 1796. The
Society now holds more than 340 portraits that form a colorful
adjunct to the core collections of personal and family papers.

Gold knee buckles of John Hancock attributed to Joseph Richardson, Jr.,
of Philadelphia, circa 1780. Provenance unknown.

Dorothy Quincy

CIRCA 1720   Portrait by an unidentified artist.
Bequest of Oliver Wendell Holmes, Jr., 1936.

Lips that lover has never kissed;
Taper fingers and slender wrist;
Hanging sleeves of stiff brocade;
So they painted the little maid.

Physician and poet Oliver Wendell Holmes was so taken with
this portrait of his great-grandmother as "a young girl in antique
costume, which made her look at first sight almost like a grown
woman," that he wrote a poem dedicated to it, "Dorothy Q:
A Family Portrait."

following pages

Phillis Wheatley

1773   Poems on Various Subjects, Religious and Moral.
Bequest of Robert Cassie Waterston, 1899.

Phillis Wheatley was eight or nine years old in 1761 when she
arrived in Boston on the slave ship *Phillis* and was sold to the
Wheatley family. She became an accomplished poet and traveled
to London, where her poems were first published in 1773. She
was freed the same year, but her early success waned and she
died in obscurity and poverty in 1784. The Historical Society
holds approximately one half of her few surviving manuscripts.

PHILLIS WHEATLEY, NEGRO SERVANT to Mr. JOHN WHEATLEY, of BOSTON.

Published according to Act of Parliament, Sept.r 1, 1773 by Arch.d Bell.
Bookseller N.o 8 near the Saracens Head Aldgate.

P O E M S

O N

VARIOUS SUBJECTS,

RELIGIOUS AND MORAL.

BY

PHILLIS WHEATLEY,

NEGRO SERVANT to Mr. JOHN WHEATLEY,
of BOSTON, in NEW ENGLAND.

L O N D O N:
Printed for A. BELL, Bookseller, Aldgate; and sold by
Meſſrs. COX and BERRY, King-Street, BOSTON.
MDCCLXXIII.

Thomas Jefferson ~ Monticello

CIRCA 1771   Plan of an observation tower.
Gift of Thomas Jefferson Coolidge, Jr., 1911.

"Architecture is my delight, and putting up and pulling down one of my favorite amusements," wrote Thomas Jefferson. Never was that more true than of his beloved home, Monticello, which he first started planning when he was twenty-four. Of more than 400 architectural drawings in the Coolidge Collection of Thomas Jefferson Manuscripts in the Historical Society, half pertain to Monticello. They bear witness to Jefferson's exquisite attention to details large and small. During his diplomatic career in Europe in the 1780s, Jefferson became a disciple of Palladio, who influenced Jefferson throughout the remainder of his life as he designed his home, the Virginia Capitol at Richmond, and the University of Virginia campus, which he considered his architectural masterpiece.

following pages

Thomas Jefferson ~ Monticello

CIRCA 1771   Final elevation of the first version.
Gift of Thomas Jefferson Coolidge, Jr., 1911.

Albert S. Southworth and Josiah J. Hawes ~ Annie Adams Fields

1853   Gift of Boylston Beale, 1941.

Photographed a year before her marriage to publisher James T. Fields in 1854, Annie Adams Fields was an author and social reformer who made her home the center of literary Boston. The Fields' circle of friends included authors published by her husband in the *Atlantic Monthly*, as well as European writers who visited Boston. In addition to her role as a literary hostess, Fields wrote biographical sketches and edited the letters of Harriet Beecher Stowe, Sarah Orne Jewett, and Celia Thaxter. The Historical Society holds her correspondence with English and American writers, and seventy volumes of her diaries and travel journals.

I wrote my journal, and
's. When I came home I
evening Kelly gordon can
us.

9   I played with Helen
front of our house, and
d time. In the even
nd   Mary we
school   I studie

school 5º I called for h
uld not come, because

Sarah Gooll Putnam ~ Diary entry

21 JANUARY 1861   Gift of Mrs. Sarah Buckminster Hayden, 1964.

Sarah Gooll Putnam, a Boston portrait artist, began her diary on Thanksgiving Day in 1860 when she was nine years old. Putnam continued her diary until her death in 1912, filling twenty-seven volumes. The diaries are richly illustrated with approximately 400 watercolor paintings and chronicle Putnam's career as an artist as well as her extensive travels throughout the United States and abroad.

There are more than 2,000 separate diaries in the Historical Society's manuscript collection, diaries that record, through the personal observations of events, the entire course of American history. There are journals kept by famous historical figures, beginning with John Winthrop's account of the founding of Massachusetts, but the strength of the collection lies in accounts of everyday life and the personal reflections of ordinary men, women, and children.

following pages

Sarah Gooll Putnam ~ Diary entries

29 NOVEMBER ~ 3 DECEMBER 1861
Gift of Mrs. Sarah Buckminster Hayden, 1964.

afternoon I played cards with Helen Paine, she lives,
or rather boards in Bowdoin street.

Friday 29th In the morning when I went to school it
was pretty snowy, and in the afternoon I did not
do much, but look at Hatty make some dancing books
Mary _____ is now painting with some oil colors, and is
paiting _____ a picture, which she is going to give to
Grand _____ mother, when it is done.

Saturday 30th In the morning when I looked out
of my window I thought the snow looked dry, but when
I was was going to school it was so sloshy that I
got my feet all wet _____, so that I asked
Miss Dimond (My _____ teacher) if I
could stand before _____ the fire, and of
course she let me, _____ with some other
girls, that were _____ wet too. I did
not go out in the _____ afternoon. Hatty
, and Mary are _____ going to the
dancing school _____ every Thursday.

89

December.

Sunday 1st of December. Christmas is coming nearer, nearer, and when it is come we shall go to cousin Jane Gray's again, and then for the weeks vacation! we shall have fun, I am going to give a good many presents, one thing I should like to have for a present would be a dictionary, and another would be a box of oil water color paints, so that I could paint pictures that looked like oil color paint, and I could paint things nicely with such paints, as   the paints that I have now are   oly water colors. As there are so   many union pictures in the   newspapers that I thought I   would paste one in here.   90   In the morning Mother and Nalty went to church, and Johnny, I stayed at home, and read. At about I stayed twelve oclock I took a walk with Mary, and Johnny down Beacon street.

91

Monday 2nd In the afternoon I stayed at home, and did not do much.

Tuesday 3rd In the morning I went with Mother to Dr Clarks to have my ear fixed, and Mother, and I had to wait a quater of an houre, before he came.

Bears Heart

Cheyenne

Bears Heart

Cheyenne Medicine

Bear's Heart ~ Buffalo Hunt

CIRCA 1876–1877   From Book of Sketches made at Fort Marion, St. Augustine, Florida. Gift of Mrs. John Forbes Perkins, 1956.

These colorful drawings, created by a Cheyenne warrior during his imprisonment in Florida after the Red River War in 1874–1875, derive from traditional Native American art and are examples of ledger art—named for the bound volumes provided by their warders in which the artists recorded camp life, hunts, and battles, as well as scenes of their imprisonment.

This volume came to Massachusetts from Florida as a token of thanks for the kindness shown to Howling Wolf, another Cheyenne captive, who came to Boston for an eye operation during his imprisonment.

Bear's Heart ~ Cheyenne Medicine Pow-wow

CIRCA 1876–1877   From Book of Sketches made at Fort Marion, St. Augustine, Florida. Gift of Mrs. John Forbes Perkins, 1956.

John Singer Sargent ~ Peter Chardon Brooks III

1890   Gift of Mrs. Levin H. Campbell and George Lewis, 2004.

John Singer Sargent was at the height of his powers when he painted this portrait of Peter Chardon Brooks III in 1890. Brooks had inherited part of the fortune of his grandfather, the Boston merchant and philanthropist Peter Chardon Brooks, and put his money to work developing Chicago real estate. In 1881, he commissioned architects Burnham & Root to design the Montauk Block, Chicago's first skyscraper. When the firm completed the taller Monadnock Building for him in 1891, it was the largest office building in the world.

The marriage of Peter Chardon Brooks III to Sarah Lawrence, the daughter of Amos Adams Lawrence, united two families long settled in New England. The marriage of their daughter, Eleanor Brooks, to Richard Middlecott Saltonstall connected the Lawrence, Brooks, and Saltonstall families—all represented in large collections of personal papers, photographs, and portraits held by the Historical Society.

About the Massachusetts Historical Society

The goal of the Historical Society's founders was "to collect, preserve and communicate materials for a complete history of this country." More than 215 years after its founding, the MHS remains faithful to its mission and at the forefront of its field.

The Massachusetts Historical Society

- provides unparalleled resources to thousands of researchers each year;

- encourages new historical scholarship through fellowships, seminars, and conferences;

- offers an extensive program of fellowships and workshops for teachers;

- publishes a range of printed and digital resources—including documentary editions, essay collections, and an annual journal;

- produces the *Adams Papers*, an authoritative edition of the correspondence, diaries, and family papers of Presidents John and John Quincy Adams;

- expands the impact of its collections through the online display of primary sources;

- sponsors an array of engaging public programs—including lectures, booksignings, and discussion series; and

- presents public exhibitions of materials from its collections and tours of its national historic landmark building.

To learn more about the Historical Society's programs and services, visit our website at www.masshist.org.

For more information on the items featured in this book, visit www.masshist.org/gallery.